Dream To Reality

Simple Strategies to Transform your Life from Ordinary to ExtraOrdinary.

Learn How to Live Your Dreams

Live Your Dreams

Turn Your Dreams To Reality Discover How You Can Achieve Anything You Want In Your Life

"The people that achieve things in life have a _clear vision_ of what they want, a _clear plan_ of how they are going to get there, and the _ability to follow this through to completion_."

I am sure you have a big dream deep in your heart that you want to become Reality? Congratulations on taking the step to achieve it with this Dream To Reality workbook Taking the first step is perhaps the most difficult thing to do.

You can become a **_super achiever_** and achieve basically any dream, vision and goals you want in your life by following the instruction set out in this workbook.

To be successful in life, takes a constant desire to learn and educate yourself AND by doing it, you will reach your goals and become a high achiever

Brian Tracy says it best...

"People with **clear**, **written goals**, accomplish far more in a **shorter period**of time than people without them could ever imagine."

You can Achieve What You Want In Life?

Become motivated today and dare to dream big Reflecting on the word of wisdom that says, "You can eat an elephant by taking one bite at a time but the key is to take the bites *early in a systematic way* and *often*. The best time to start is *now* and you have the tool in your hand to **Turn Your Dream To Reality**

I look forward to seeing you at the top

To your success

BibiApampa

www.BibiApampa.org

ABOUT THE AUTHOR

Bibi Bunmi Apampa– Managing Director of The Empowerment Centre and successful Entrepreneur, Chartered Accountant, Author, International speaker, Wealth Strategist, Business Coach and Trainer.

She is a valued fellow of the prestigious accountancy organizations, including the Institute of Chartered Accountants and Chartered Institute of taxation.

The Empowerment Centre and The QueenMakers Academy was set up by her to help and empower ordinary people improve their lives, not only financially, but also physically, personally, professionally and spiritually.

Through her Training, Mentoring, Speaking and Coaching programs, She has empowered many people over the years to Start and Grow their own businesses, Build wealth, create multiple streams of income and achieve financial independence.

She can be contacted through her website at www.BibiApampa.org or on facebook at www.facebook.com/bapampa email MyBusinessCoach@live.com

Dream To Reality

Life Planner Contents

7 areas	The Seven Steps to go from Deam to Reality are:
➢ Family and Relationships ➢ Personal Development ➢ Career and Business ➢ Money and Investments ➢ Social and Recreation ➢ Health and Fitness ➢ Spiritual	1. Write the Vision - Find your Purpose and Catch the Vision, Create a vision board 2. Goal setting - Analyse your current reality, Set Goals Do stock taking. 3. What is the way forward - write out the different options 4. Follow A MAP (Mindset, Action, Process)– Break it down step by step 5. What leverage can you use to accomplish the Vision 6. Build a mastermind Team to help you accomplish the Vision 7. Be grateful for the vision, Believe in the Vision, Visualize the Vision, Run with the Vision, Hang on to the Vision

1. Introduction   2pgs
2. Dream To Reality Worksheet   1pg
3. How to create A Vision Board   1pg
4. Goal Setting Worksheet   8pgs
5. Goal – Reality – Option worksheet   2pgs
6. The art of Gratitude worksheet   1pg
7. 7 Steps to Wealth Acceleration and Success   2pgs
8. Monthly Productivity Planner   12copies
9. Time Management   2pgs
10. Easy and Fun ways to incorporate fitness
     into busy schedules   1pg
11. Stress Management   2pgs

BONUS

Become An Expert – Build Authority, Celebrity and Expert Status

Become the Expert in a Niche   1pg
Positioning as an Expert   2pgs
Building your Brand   3pgs
Fast strategic business plan   1pg
10 ways to grow your business   2pgs

Dream to Reality

Transform your life from Ordinary to ExtraOrdinary

www.DreamToReality.eu

Summary

The Seven Steps to go from Dream to Reality are:

1. Write the Dream - Find your Purpose, Catch the Dream, Create a Vision board
2. Goal setting   - Analyse your current reality, Set Goals Do stock taking.
3. What is the way forward - write out the different options
4. Follow A MAP (Mindset, Action, Process)– Break it down step by step
5. Explore the different leverage available to accomplish the Dream
6. Build a mastermind Team to help you accomplish the Dream
7. Be grateful for the Dream, Believe in the Dream, Visualise the Dream, Run with the Dream, Hang on to the Dream

The Seven Steps to go from Dream to Reality are:

1. Write the Dream - Find your Purpose, Catch the Dream, Create a Dream board
   - ➢ Please go through and follow the instructions on the Goal setting workshop, **Goals to Reality worksheet** and how to create a Dream board
2. Goal setting   - Analyse your current reality, Set Goals Do stock taking.
   - ➢ Read through everything you've written on your **Goal setting worksheets** and reflect. What do you need to do to go from Reality to Goal?
3. What is the way forward - write out the different options available that comes to mind whether you think they are achievable or not using the **Goal – Reality – Options Worksheet**

7

4. Follow A MAP – Break it down step by step

   ➢ Mindset – Your mindset from now on is important. You need to have a positive mental attitude. No matter what goes on around it must not dampen your attitude. This will involve

   ✓   what you think and focus on
   ✓   what you say,
   ✓   what you do while waiting for the accomplishment of your Dream

   ➢ Action – You will remain the same person you are today in five years times except for two things. The books you read and the people you relate with. In looking at the actions you need to take for your Dream to become reality, Consider

   ✓   steps you need to take,
   ✓   training you need to acquire,
   ✓   people you need to meet
   ✓   books you need to read that will enlighten you

   ➢ Process - You'll need to put in a <u>Structure</u> and <u>Support</u> system which involves:

   ✓   SYSTEM or STRATEGY you will need to follow
   ✓   MENTOR / COACH – success leaves clues, who is successful in your niche or area of specialization that you can model
   ✓   NETWORK – which network do you need to join or build – association, social media, club,
   ✓   TEAM – who are the people that you need on your team to make it easier to accomplish your Dream
   ✓   SKILLS & TOOLS – what are the equipments or tools that you need to acquire

5. Explore the different leverage available to accomplish the

> - OPM – Other People's Money
> - OPI – Other People's Idea
> - OPE – Other People's Effort
> - OPT – Other People's Time
> - OPW – Other People's Work

6. Build a mastermind TEAM to help you Accomplish the Dream – Together Everybody Achieves More

> - Manage the Team
> - Foster Innovation and creativity

7. Be grateful for the Dream, Believe in the Dream, Visualise the Dream, Run with the Dream, Hang on to the Dream
> - Practice the attitude of gratitude daily – the more gratitude you deliberately think and feel, the more abundance you'll receive and the nearer you'll be to the realization of your Dream
> - Work on the **Attitude of Gratitude Worksheet**
> - On a daily basis go through your
>   > - Dream to Reality worksheet
>   > - The Dream Board
>   > - Attitude of Gratitude Worksheet

Remember the Dream is yours Go For it

HOW DO YOU EXPAND YOUR DREAM

1. Idealise – the kind of life you want.
2. Verbalise – positive affirmations in personal, positive present tense.
3. Visualise – the successful state, situation through mental rehearsal.
4. Emotionalise – i.e. create the feeling of pride, joy, satisfaction and pleasure.
5. Realise – Not being afraid of the space between your dreams and reality if you can conceive it, believe it, you can achieve it.

LIVING IN YOUR DREAM

Living in **your Dream** involves having the following **PERSONAL TRAITS**.

1. **Long term DREAM mentality** : Ability to see what others cannot see.

2. **COURAGE**: Ability to act despite tremendous doubt.

3. **CREATIVITY**: Ability to think outside the box.

4. **WITHSTAND CRITICISM**: Ability to stand and continue despite criticism.

5. **DELAY GRATIFICATION**: Ability to wait, sow and delay gratification till full harvest.

REMEMBER THE FOLLOWING LAWS THAT WILL MAKE YOU UNSTOPPABLE

1. Law of Belief – As a man thinks in his heart so is he.
2. Law of Expectation – Whatever you expect with confidence will become yourself fulfilling prophesy.
3. Law of Attraction – You are a living magnet, and you attract people and circumstances that are consistent with your dominant thoughts.
4. Law of Correspondence – Your outer world is a reflection of your inner world. It is a reflection of what is going on inside you
5. Law of Karma – Sowing and Reaping
6. Law of Forgiveness
7. Law of compensation

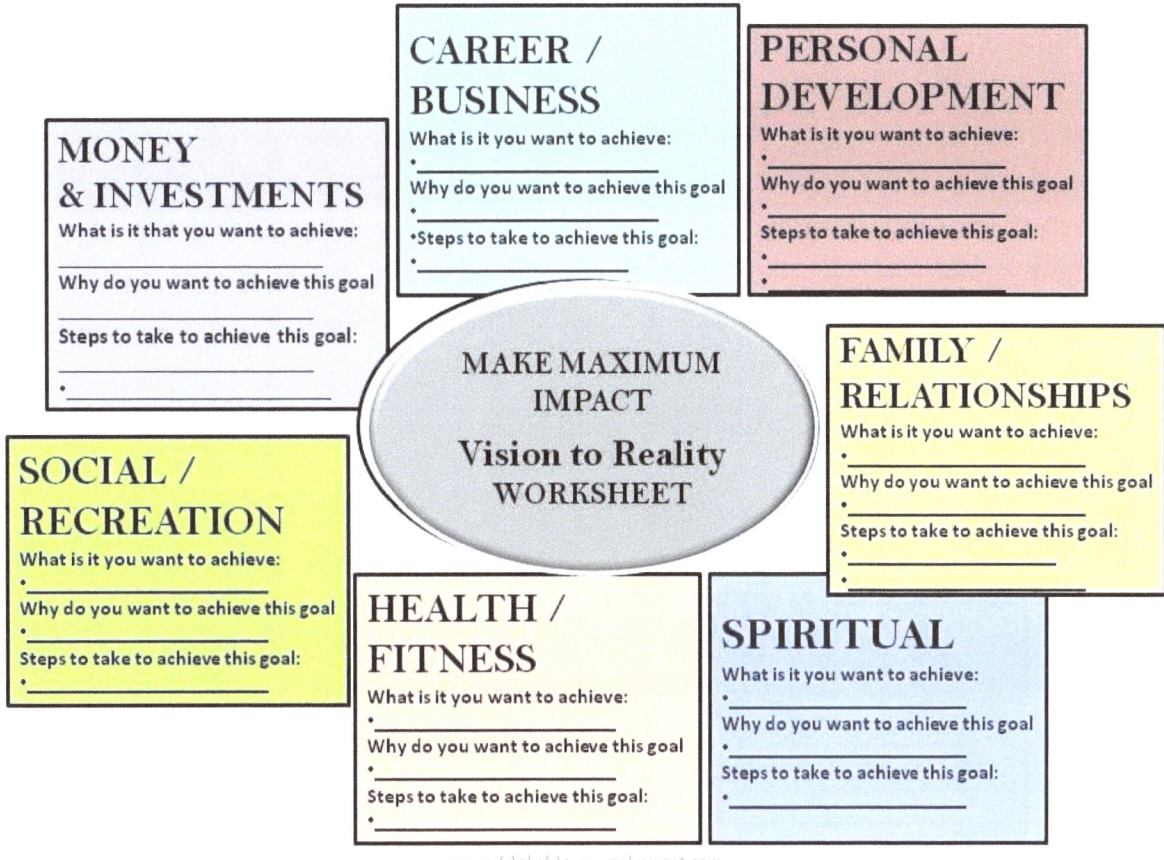

How to use the Vision to Reality Worksheet and Goal Setting Worksheet

1. Start brainstorming ALL the things you want to achieve in your life : everything you want to do, everything you want to have, everything you want to be. Write them down in the Goal setting worksheet

2. Make sure you cover **all** areas of life

3. Remember you are brainstorming. Don't question, don't judge, don't censor, just keep writing. In fact **don't let the pen stop moving!**

4. In psychology there is something called the "Corridor principle" what it states is that " when a big door opens, other smaller doors will open

5. Now go through your list and pick the major goal under the Seven categories that if accomplished would make the other smaller goals achievable
6. Write this major goal in the Vision to Reality worksheet under the different categories and why it is important for you to achieve this goal.
7. The purpose for wanting to achieve this goal must be "greater than you" ie it must be a vision that would make your existence on earth meaningful and worth while
8. Write down one step you can take immediately towards the achievement of this major goal

How to Make a Vision Board

Made famous by The Secret, Oprah Winfrey, and the Law of Attraction, vision boards can be a great way to visualize your goals and what you want to accomplish with your life. In short, a vision board is a collage of images that are in line with your dreams and desires, helping to encourage positive feelings and a sense of inspiration. So, how do you make one?

First, decide on what you want to accomplish with your vision board. It could be a general collection of images and affirmations for your life in its entirety, including both your professional and your personal life. Alternatively, your vision board could be focused on one or two more specific goals. Both options have their relative strengths and advantages.

Second, find corresponding images and phrases that are in line with the theme of your vision board. These can be found by clipping magazines, going through your old photo collections or by browsing the Internet.

Third, include affirmations that will remind you of the goals of your vision board. These key words and phrases will help you stay on track and keep a positive outlook. This is a big part of the Law of Attraction.

Fourth, arrange your affirmations and images on your vision board in a way that makes sense to you. Some people prefer a more random collage, whereas others like a greater level of organization.

Fifth, place your vision board somewhere that you'll see it every day. If you don't see your vision board, it won't do what it's meant to do

And **finally**, take a picture of your vision board, save it as your display picture on your phone and screen saver on all your digital devices so that you can look at it everyday

Given that we are fully in the digital age, a physical vision board may not be as easy or appropriate as it may have been in the past. Instead, you may consider a "virtual" or digital vision board using Powerpoint or Paint. Just be sure to follow the same principles and look at your vision board image daily.

Download pictures from the internet that are in line with your vision. Paste the images on a powerpoint slide Arrange them with affirmations in a way that makes sense to you. Save the image as a jpeg image and use as your display picture and screen saver

PERSONAL GOAL SETTING

STEP 1. GOAL	Decide what you want and write it down clearly in the present tense.	
STEP 2. WHEN	Set deadline. Set sub deadlines if you want the more specific, the more you will accomplish	*Date:* *Activity:*
STEP 3. CHALLENGES	Determine the obstacles	
STEP 4. LEARN	Determine what you must learn. To do something you have never done before, you must become someone you have never been before. Every new goal requires you to become a new person	
STEP 5. HELP	Who do you want to help you? What will you have to do to earn their support? What is in it for them?	
STEP 6 PLAN	Make a plan to achieve your goal. Organise the list according to priority.	
STEP 7. ACTION	TAKE ACTION! DO something each day that moves you toward achievement of your goal. Develop the momentum principle.	

NOTE : TYPES OF GOALS

1. Family / Relationship Goals
2. Career / Business Goals
3. Personal Development Goals
4. Money / Investment Goals
5. Health & Fitness Goals
6. Social / Recreation Goals
7. Spiritual Goals

STEPS

1. Decide Exactly what you want
2. Set a deadline for your goals
3. Determine the obstacles you have to overcome to achieve your goals
4. Determine the additional knowledge, skills & abilities that you will need
5. Determine the people, groups and organizations whose help you will need to achieve your goals
6. make detailed plans to achieve the Goals
7. Take action

GOALSETTING WORKSHEET			
FAMILY GOALS	LIFETIME	10 YEARS	1 YEAR
➤			
➤			
➤			
➤			
➤			

CAREER/ BUSINESS GOALS	LIFETIME	10 YEARS	1 YEAR
➢			
➢			
➢			
➢			
PERSONAL DEVELOPMENT GOALS	LIFETIME	10 YEARS	1 YEAR
➢			
➢			
➢			
EDUCATION GOALS	LIFETIME	10 YEARS	1 YEAR
➢			
➢			
➢			
➢			

16

MONEY / INVESTMENT GOALS	LIFETIME	10 YEARS	1 YEAR
➤			
➤			
➤			
➤			
RELATIONSHIP GOALS	LIFETIME	10 YEARS	1 YEAR
➤			
➤			
➤			
➤			
HEALTH / FITNESSGOALS	LIFETIME	10 YEARS	1 YEAR
➤			
➤			
➤			

RECREATION AND ADVENTURE GOALS	LIFETIME	10 YEARS	1 YEAR
➢			
➢			
➢			
SOCIAL GOALS	LIFETIME	10 YEARS	1 YEAR
➢			
➢			
➢			
SPIRITUAL GOALS	LIFETIME	10 YEARS	1 YEAR
➢			
➢			
➢			

Top Five Things You Want To Do

1.

2.

3.

4.

5.

Top Five Things You Want To Accomplish

1.

2.

3.

4.

5.

Top Five Things You Want To Have

1.

2.

3.

4.

5.

Top Five Things You Want To Learn

1.

2.

3.

4.

5.

Top Five People You Want To Meet

1.

2.

3.

4.

5.

Top Five People You Want To Have Dinner With

1.

2.

3.

4.

5.

Top Five People You Want To Thank

1.

2.

3.

4.

5.

Top Five Mentors

1.

2.

3.

4.

5.

Top Five Places You Want To See

1.

2.

3.

4.

5.

Top Five Places You Want To Experience

1.

2.

3.

4.

5.

Top Five Places You Want To Live

1.

2.

3.

4.

5.

Top Five Foods You Want To Eat

1.

2.

3.

5.

Top Five Jobs You Want To Have

1.

2.

3.

4.

5.

Top Five Businesses You Want To Start

1.

2.

3.

4.

5.

Top Five Career Titles You Want

1.

2.

3.

4.

5.

Top Five People You Want To Work For

1.

2.

3.

4.

5.

Top Five Books You Want To Read

1.

2.

3.

4.

5.

Top Five People You Want To Impact

1.

2.

3.

4.

5.

Top Five Things You Want To Give

1.

2.

3.

4.

5.

Top Five Things You Want To Be Remembered For

1.

2.

3.

4.

5.

Dream to Reality

Transform your life from Ordinary to ExtraOrdinary

Goal – Reality – Options Worksheet

Write out detailed information about your Goals and current situation. There are seven main areas but we will concentrate on **FINANCES, RELATIONSHIPS, HEALTH** and **FITNESS.**

Note **Goal* – What you would like to Achieve, Where you want to go

   *Reality – Your current situation and position

   *Options – The various options to move from Reality to Goal that comes to mind whether you think they are achievable or not

FINANCES – Money & Investments, Business & Career, Personal Development, Retirement Planning, Estate Planning

	GOAL	*REALITY*	*OPTIONS*
1.			
2.			
3.			

What is the one thing which if I can do very well, focus on or have will enable me achieve the biggest Goal in my finances

RELATIONSHIPS – Family, Marital, Spiritual, Social & Community Activities

GOAL	_REALITY_	_OPTIONS_

1.

2.

3.

What is the one thing which if I can do very well, focus on or have will enable me achieve my biggest Goal in my Relationships

HEALTH & FITNESS – Diet, Weight Loss, Fitness, Exercise, Healthy Eating

GOAL	_REALITY_	_OPTIONS_

1.

2.

3.

What is the one thing which if I can do very well, Focus on or have will enable me achieve the biggest Goal for my health and fitness

> **Remember –** The Reason many People fail is broken FOCUS
>
> **F**ollow **O**ne **C**ourse **U**ntil **S**uccessful

MY IDEAL DAILY SUCCESS ROUTINE

What should I incorporate into my lifestyle DAILY to enable me achieve my goals

This should incorporate activities relating to FINANCES, RELATIONSHIPS, HEALTH and **FITNESS**

1 --

2 --

3 --

4 --

5 --

6 --

7 --

Dream to Reality

Transform your life from Ordinary to ExtraOrdinary

The Attitude of Gratitude Worksheet

In the book "The Magic " by Rhonda Byrne she wrote down the steps to take in expressing gratitude to enable you achieve your visions and dreams

1. Count your blessings: make a list of ten blessings you are grateful for
2. Write why you are grateful for each blessing
3. Reread your list, and at the end of each blessing say thank you, thank you, thank you,
4. Feel as grateful for that blessing as you can
5.

   We will adapt it for our **Dream to Reality** exercise

➢ Family and Relationships – Blessing I'm grateful for and why?

   Blessing: _____

   Why I'm Grateful:_____

➢ Personal Development – Blessing I'm grateful for and why?

   Blessing: _____

   Why I'm Grateful: _____

➢ Career and Business – Blessing I'm grateful for and why?

Blessing: _____

Why I'm Grateful: _____

➢ Money and Investments – Blessing I'm grateful for and why?

Blessing: _____

Why I'm Grateful: _____

➢ Social and Recreation – Blessing I'm grateful for and why?

Blessing: _____

Why I'm Grateful: _____

➢ Health and Fitness – Blessing I'm grateful for and why?

Blessing: _____

Why I'm Grateful: _____

➢ Spiritual – Blessing I'm grateful for and why?

Blessing: _____

Why I'm Grateful: _____

7 Steps to Wealth Acceleration and Success

1. Model a Successful Person

Success leaves clues. Don't copy but model. Look at about 3 successful people in your niche and take up the positive aspect of their program / routine and model your own after it

2. Get Healthy - Health is Wealth. It's easy just EAT

E - Eat Differently - diet fitness

A - Act Differently - body fitness

T - Think Different - lifestyle fitness

3. Overcome Fear - Face your Giants

FEAR is False Evidence Appearing Real

Fear of the future, fear of failure, fear of rejection - face your giants

The Enemy you refuse to fight today will come back to fight you and your children.

4. Make better use of your time 80:20 principle

What is the 20% activity that will give 80% result
Two things are Levellers
    Time - we all have 24 hours
    Education - get educated to increase your ability.

There are 24 hours in a day, let us look at extreme use of time
8hrs to sleep
8hrs at work
2hrs to commute
3hrs to play
2hrs to eat
Total 23hrs leaves you with 1 hour - you can claim an extra hour either by sleeping 1hour later or wake up1hour earlier
One hour times 5days times 50weeks times 3years will put you at the top of your field, in 5years a national Authority and in 7 years, you can be one of the best people in the world at what you do

5. Value and Build Empowering Relationships.

a. Your value system is important - integrity, dream/ goal, peace, purpose, passion, patience,

b. Relationships hierarchy - God, Spouse, Children, others

c. Get a mentor / coach. Become accountable to somebody. Leave a legacy

Build Empowering Relationships
1. Show a genuine interest in people.
2. Listen to them.
3. Believe in them.
4. Inspire them.
5. Make them feel important.
6. Be a role model for them.
7. Challenge them.
8. Spend time with them.
9. See their point of view.
10. Praise them for their successes

6. Take Risks

If you don't take risks now you'll be at risk later.

Become an Entrepreneur. Build streams of income that will move you more from Earned Income to Passive and Residual Income

There are Four Money Mountains. Learn how to create wealth

- - Real Estate, Paper Assets, Business, Expert Infopreneur.

Remember most Millionaires keep their money in Real Estate as it always appreciates overtime

7. Acquire the Seven Money Skills

- **Value money** – miracle of compound interest $100 a month over 45yrs is $1million
- **Make money** - The rich don't work for money they know have to make money work for them. The key to great wealth is a person's ability to convert Earned Income into Passive and Portfolio Income as quickly as possible
- **Save money** - 80/20 Principle – 10% to God, 10% to pay yourself and live within the remaining 80%
- **Invest money** – Invest in 3 Money mountains Real state, Portfolio investment, Your business
- **Manage money** – Acquire Good Financial planning skills
- **Share money** – Sow & be a Giver
- **Protect / shield money –** its not how much you make, its how much you keep, learn how to legally minimise tax while protecting your assets

Maximum Impact

Monthly Productivity Planner

PRIORITIES - The main things I must complete this month, no matter what.

List the priorities and to-dos that must be accomplished this month and Do these before getting trapped in your inbox and other people's agendas.

1. _____	6. _____
2_____	7. _____
3. _____	8. _____
4. _____	9. _____
5. _____	10._____

PEOPLE

People I need to reach out to this month	People I'm waiting on this month.
List the people you have to reach out to this month no matter what:	List the people who you need something from to move forward:
1._____	1._____
2_____	2_____
3._____	3._____
4._____	4._____
5._____	5._____

PROJECTS

Project #1:_____	Project #2:_____	Project #3:_____
5 big things I must do to move this project forward:	5 big things I must do to move this project forward:	5 big things I must do to move this project forward:
1. _____	1. _____	1. _____
2. _____	2. _____	2. _____
3. _____	3. _____	3. _____
4. _____	4. _____	4. _____
5. _____	5. _____	5. _____

** Make 12 copies of this page one for each month

TIME MANAGEMENT

- **7 laws of Time Management**
- **7 facts you should know about Managing your Time**
- **7 tips in making your Time count.**

7 laws of Time Management

Everything you are today and everything you become in the future will be determined by the way you think and the way you use your time. Your attitude towards time is a critical factor in all you do and everything you accomplish. The laws of time management are timeless and eternal. They work everywhere and for everyone, When you align your activities in harmony with these laws and principles, you will begin to accomplish vastly more than you ever thought possible.

1. **The Law of Priorities –** *Your ability to set clear and accurate priorities on your time determines the entire quality of your life.* The Pareto principle says that 20% of your activities will account for 80% of the value of your activities. Thus means that if you have a list of ten items to accomplish, two of those will be worth more than the other eight items altogether. To achieve great things Prioritise your activities and concentrate on the 20% that will give you 80% result. Do this by writing out what you need to get done in a day, "A to-do List" and prioritise the most important on the list that will give you the most result.

2. **The Law of Planning –** *Every minute spent in planning saves ten minutes in execution.* It only takes 10 -12 minutes for you to make a plan for your day. This investment of 10-12minutes will save you 100-120 minutes in execution. This is an increase in productive time of approximately two hours per day or a 25% increase in productivity and performance

3. **The Law of Timing & Sequentiality –** *Time management enables you to control the timing and the sequence of events in your life and thereby enable you to take complete control of your life*. You decide to do certain things before you do others, by making new choices and better decisions, you put your hands on the wheel of your life and steer it in the direction that you really want to go

4. **The law of Leverage-** *Archimedes the Greek philosopher once said "Give me a lever long enough and a place to stand and I can move the world"* Develop your ability to pull together other people's effort **OPE** other people's knowledge **OPK** and other people's money **OPM**, other people's ideas **OPI** you can accomplish vastly more in the same period of time than someone who is forced to rely on his or her own personal energy and resources

5. **The Law of Timeliness –** *The ability to act faster than anyone else can be your greatest asset.* Time is the currency of the 21st century. Your ability to set priorities and then to move fast and get the job done quickly and well is the most valued set of time management skills in the workplace,

6. **The Law of Practice –** *Continuous practice of a skill reduced the time required to perform the task and increase the output achieved.* The more you practice a key skill the less time it takes you to perform the same task.

7. **The Law of Time pressure –** *There is never enough time to do everything, but there is always enough time to do the most important things*. Parkinson's Law says "Work expands to fill the time allotted for it" however the reverse is also true. Work contracts to fill the time allotted to it" use this law by setting deadlines for yourself that forces you to complete tasks on time

7 facts you should know about Managing your Time

1. **Anything Significant in your life will require the investment of time**. Invest time in your "Love Circle" those you love and whose activities affect your life e.g. family, mentors/mentees, close friends and staff

2. **Time Invested in Preparation will repay you a thousand times over**. Jesus referred to those who took the time to invest in the foundation of a house on a rock were wise.

3. **Your attitude toward time is revealed every time you make an appointment with someone**. Punctuality sends a message – Time matters to me.

4. **Successful negotiations will always require the investment of time** – those who overcome the temptation to hurry.. always control the transaction

5. **It is your responsibility to train those around you to respect your time** – you do so by respecting their own time as well

6. **Time invested in Rest and Restoration of your energy will reduce tour stress level**- take time out to rest and refresh yourself, Jesus always took time out to rest and in retreat

7. **Invest time in your personal "ME-time" diet, physical fitness and body exercise** – Do not abuse your body it is the temple of God, Eat right, exercise at least 30mins daily, remove self from stressors or remove stressors from self, Blessed is the person who is too busy to worry in the daytime and too sleepy to worry at night, Maintain positive attitude, act positively towards people, and do not react to the negativity of others

7 tips in making your Time count

There are 24 hours in a day let us look at extreme use of time
8hrs to sleep
8hrs at work
2hrs to commute
3hrs to play
2hrs to eat

Total 23hrs leaves you with 1 hour - you can claim an extra hour either by sleeping 1hour later or wake up1hour earlier

One hour times 5days times 50weeks times 3years will put you at the top of your field, in 5years a national Authority and in 7 years, you can be one of the best people in the world at what you do

Tips

1. Focus on carefully planning the next 24 hours, 7days, next 30 days, 1 year, etc your Goals, personal development, career and business development
2. Schedule quiet time with God in prayer, praise and worship for wisdom, guidance and direction.
3. Schedule time to Monitor, Mentor and Motivate your "Love Circle"
4. Schedule time for restoration – A nap or simply relaxing, winding down and distressing yourself
5. Schedule time for body exercise- it keeps you alert, healthy, focused and extends your life span
6. Guard access to yourself – qualify those who enter your arena of life. Avoid time wasting friends, They must desire what you possess or must possess something you desire.
7. Unclutter your life by uncluttering your day. Eliminate the things God did not specifically tell you to do. Live a simple life

Recognizing and Respecting the miracle gift of time will multiply your productivity, Increase your financial worth and make every moment of relationships valued.

Easy and Fun ways to Incorporate Fitness into busy Schedules

If you have a sitting job, stand up and stretch yourself every half an hour. Most of the jobs today are indeed sitting jobs that are in one word sedentary. This is especially true for those who sit and punch away at the keyboard or toy with the mouse all day long. While making telephone calls try walking up and down

Use the stairs instead of the elevator whenever you can. Instead of waddling up and down the staircase, try taking them two at a time. Now this is something that you have to be careful about because we do not want you to trip. So when you do this make sure that your feet are well and truly planted on each step before you increase the beat and try two at a time.

Any distance is walkable if you have the time, so consider walking to places that you would normally drive (such as work or the market if they're not too far away). It may take you longer, but the health benefits will last you a lifetime. Get down at a block before your destination and walk the rest of the way. You might not have time to fit in long walks in your busy schedule so this is one way of ensuring that you at least get to walk for a little bit every day. If you take the bus or the subway, get down at an earlier station and see if you can walk the rest of the way. If you drive to work, see if you can get space in a parking lot that is a little away from your office.

When nobody is watching try doing pelvic gyrations. If you take a moment to observe it you will see that it is the mid section of our body that gets the least bit of exercise and that is probably why the signs of weight gain are mostly seen there. It is the same reason why we find it very difficult to lose weight in that section. So the best thing that you can do is consciously try to give that part a little bit of exercise. Stomach crunches might be too strenuous an exercise to start off with but gyrations are relatively mild.

Pelvic gyrations make you thrust your midsection towards all directions and this is the best way of *tightening every muscle in that mid section and that is of course what weight loss is all about.* Turn on music and dance like wild. Let your hair down once in a while. Go back to the days of wild child hood
.

Tuck in your tummy whenever you walk. Get that proper gait. And the best way for that is to tuck in your tummy and inflate your chest. Do not let your tummy hang above your belt line like some unruly layer of flesh. Bring it under the belt. Each time you tuck in your tummy, you will feel the pressure on the muscles of your stomach. This tightening and loosening of these muscles is even better than stomach crunches.

Try breathing exercises. You might be surprised to know that breathing exercises too can lead to weight loss. If you are doing the breathing exercises properly, you will find that you can exert a lot of pressure on the muscles around the mid section. You can feel a tightening of these muscles each time you breathe in or breathe out. So go ahead and breathe properly, it is good for you.
Breathe in air as strongly as you can and as you do so, tuck in your tummy as much as you can. Hold it like this for a few seconds (count to 20) and then slowly release your breath taking care not to let out your tummy. Try to keep breathing like this at least fifty or sixty times in a day.

Try massaging your partner. This is a fun way to lose weight. It is something that can give your partner a lot of pleasure and at the same time can give you a lot of exertion there by leading to weight loss.The attitude over here should of course be you scratch my back I will scratch yours. It should not be a one sided effort or else the interest will soon dwindle. In fact it is a good idea if couple take up weight loss routines together. They can keep watch over each other, help control those urges to eat and motivate each other to stick to the routine.

Do not slouch in your chair but try to maintain an erect posture with your tummy tucked in. Slouching is a very bad habit. Not only is it bad for your back but it also gives you a very flabby figure. Make it a point to always sit as erect as you can. It is also a terrific way to ward off back problems.

❖ Stress Management Techniques

The goal is to remove self from stressors or remove stressors from self

1. Relationship

- ✓ Keep away from people you don't enjoy who drain your energy or belittle you or your accomplishment.
- ✓ Spend plenty time with a few friends you enjoy (trustworthy friends).
- ✓ Keep updating the list of why you love your spouse.

2. Diet

- ✓ Take a balanced diet
- ✓ Avoid sugar, fat and oil
- ✓ Avoid smoking and alcohol

3. Exercise

- ✓ Adequate physical exercise is the single greatest stress reducer known
- ✓ Walking is a relaxed form of exercise. Incorporate a 30min daily walk into your lifestyle
- ✓ Swimming is good
- ✓ Jogging
- ✓ When exercising Endorphin is released which boost energy helping to cope with stress

4. Water

- ✓ Has been used naturally to cure many diseases
- ✓ Helps eliminate toxins and metabolites in the body which are known stressors
- ✓ It is widely recommended that you take 1.5 litres of water 3 times daily.

5. Sleep

✓ Blessed is the person who is too busy to worry in the daytime and too sleepy to worry at night.
✓ Learn to sleep. The rule is, stay heavy in bed, sink deep into sleep.
✓ A Little carbohydrate 30 min before bed removes cases of insomnia
✓ Early to bed, early to rise, makes a man healthy, wealthy and wise.
✓ Sleep before 10pm, wake before 7am

6. Relaxation exercises

✓ Going for walks
✓ Reading for pleasure
✓ Listening to music – changing the atmosphere of the environment
✓ Taking a bath
✓ Meditation
✓ Deep breathing exercise

7. Way of life

✓ Maintain positive attitude, act positively towards people, and do not react to the negativity of others.
✓ Faith: The beginning of stress is the end of faith and The beginning of faith is the end of stress
✓ Humility: The humbler you are, the less your level of stress
✓ Forgiveness: forgiveness saves the expense of anger, the cost of hatred, the waste of a spirit. Forgiveness warms the heart and cools the sting. Learn to forgive
✓ Giving: Endorphin is released when you share with someone in need. The more you give the less stressed you become.
✓ Laughter: laughter is jogging for the intestine. Learn to laugh. Laugh like a child
✓ Love: love yourself, love your neighbours
✓ Thankfulness/Gratitude: the best attitude is gratitude. This guarantees a happy state of mind.
✓ Positive expectation: Always assume that things will turn out well in the final analysis.

✓ Reducing Caffeine intake will help to manage anxiety

✓ Smoking cessation is important as nicotine is a stimulant

8. Skin

✓ Cream your skin

✓ Massage if possible

❖ Helps excretion of metabolites, toxins which are known stressors

❖ Helps keep the skin healthy to wade off invading organisms or germs

9. Vacation: Carefully planned holiday helps manage stress

✓ Take holidays at least 2-4 weeks every year

✓ Go on a retreat to recharge or a vacation to distress and rest

10. Use of Pareto Principle/Law of Least Effort/Law of Vital few or trivial many.

✓ Be friendly with few friends intimately

✓ Do more of less- delegate the rest

✓ Be the best in less – leave the rest

✓ Know more about less- become an expert

✓ Never take your job home.

Conclusion: Stress is the darkroom where negatives are developed. Mere thinking will not overcome it, but knowledge backed up by positive, constructive actions will do the trick. Stress does not empty tomorrow of its sorrow; it empties today of its strength.

Building your Business to Become "The Expert" in a niche

Create Authority, Celebrity and Expert Status

Recommended Training program at www.MakeMaximumImpact.com

How Do you become "The Expert"

- Know your Niche and your Micro Niche
- Develop your Perfect Pitch – elevator speech
- Master your topic & Become an authority- study, train, network, join association, write articles, build niche website, model success
- Become a Published Author
- Create your products – Book, Cds, DVDs, Produce an information product
- Become "Web Famous"– www.BecomeWebFamous.net
- Become a Speaker with a magnetic Personality
- Get into Joint Ventures and Partnerships
- Link with Multiple websites

Five Strategies

- Choose your topic
- Choose your audience – who you want to teach eg women, children, entrepreneurs, couples, white collar workers, corporate executives
- Choose your vehicle – book, speaking, training seminars, coaching, internet
- Choose your marketing strategy
- Consistently promote – offline and online

Building your "Experts Empire"

- Do not undervalue what you know
- Choose your topic and dig deep
- Breakdown information into step by step process - Create frameworks and products eg 7habits, 30 tips,
- Focus on three things **– Distinction, Excellence and Service**
- Model success – Success leaves clues, Find leaders in your niche and study and follow them, sign up to be on their mailing list

Being successful as an Expert

- **Position** yourself intelligently as the expert
- **Package** your information so people can buy
- **Promote** yourself strategically and consistently
- **Partner** with others to get your message out

Recommended Training program at www.MakeMaximumImpact.com

Positioning as an Expert
Targeting Your Niche

A niche business is a business that is targeting one very specific group of people with a very specific common shared interest or passion or desire. A target market / niche is the group of people you've decided to help. You can narrow it down to age, occupation, gender, location etc,

The key to successful niche marketing is to **pick a niche small enough to dominate, and large enough to be profitable**

Conditions for a Hot Niche Market

• It contains a large number of people

• These people are irrationally passionate

• They have disposable income

• They have their own jargon

• They have their own magazines

• They may hold their own conferences and events

• They have their own celebrities

• looking for a subculture or a tribe

Where to find hot markets

1. Magazines (magazines.com)

2. Bookstores (Amazon.com)

3. Digital Market Places (Clickbank / PayDotCom)

4. Talking to Passionate People

5. Listening to People's Problems

6. Watching TV

Arriving at the Right niche idea for you

Important factors to consider

1. Your Passion - What you find fascinating & love to learn about
2. What you love doing – People compliment you or ask your advice
3. What you've always wanted to learn
4. What you have been through in life
5. Your Legacy – if you were to die, what message would you want to communicate to the world
6. What are you willing to speak about – Live and breathe for the next 5years. What really inspires and engages you
7. As a Child what did you really want to be
8. What is your biggest dream
9. If money was not an issue what would you be doing
10. If you couldn't fail or forced to start over again what would you do

It might also be:

- a gap in the market that you can fill
- a business related to the work you do already
- an interest or hobby that you can turn into a business

Other factors to consider

- How big is the market for this product or service?
- How easy will it be to run this business?
- Are members of this market willing AND able to PAY for information relating to this area?
- How easy will it be to sell to customers?
- Will it stand out from the crowd?
- Will it make enough profit to live on?

BUILDING YOUR BRAND

Personal Branding is about building a tribe of Raving Fans – A true fan is defined as someone who will purchase anything and everything you produce.

Step 1 – know your Audience

What does your target market want? What frustrates them the most?

Step 2 – Define your position

Branding is all about positioning and being the problem solver – what specific solution do you want to be known for as "The Guru – go to person?

Step 3 – Create the Solution

Create a product or service that gives them what they want

Step 4 – Content

It is your content that will attract people to you and will assist in establishing your authority position. Attract first then engage producing high quality content that your audience finds valuable

Step 5 – Promotion

You should always have a promotional campaign in motion

Step 6 – Over Deliver Strive to exceed client's expectations

How To Build Your Brand

Process

1.   Choose Your Niche → Expertise, Brand, area of Specialization
2.   Pick your audience - target market - who you want to serve – Woman, Business men, teenagers, Doctors, narrow down your niche
3.   Discover their need – problem to be solved and create the solution at different price levels
4.   Read Widely about your area of specialization and Learn how to write articles on your niche area – Dedicate 1hr a day 5 times a week to reading about your specialized area
5.   Build your website / blog and load with quality content to start building your brand
6.   Create Social Media Networks – facebook fan page, Twitter, LinkedIn,
7.   Create your Youtube channel –
8.   Write Articles an "your brand" and submit to print media and article submission service on the internet
9.   Convert your articles to "How To" videos upload to your Youtube channel
10. Write and Publish your book on your area of specialization / niche area in different formats – ebook, Amazon Kindle, Paper Back
11. Learn how to Become a Great Speaker and motivator with a magnetic personality and create at least 5 keynote speeches and seminars on your area of specialization that you can deliver whenever called upon
12. Excel at networking and building relationships
13. Volunteer to speak at events on your brand/niche
14. Create your Demo DVD – You speaking/Teaching on "your brand" and upload to your Youtube channel distribute to other video networks
15. Create your Products – You Speaking & Teaching on "your broad" on CD, MP3, DVD

16. Grant media interviews and press Releases on "Your Brand" featuring your book and other products

17. Publish Testimonials of your book and other products on your website and social media properties

18. Build a list of raving fans and followings using your Facebook fan page and Twitter page

19. Partner with other Experts in your specialized area and push your brand into "Joint Venture" relationships

20. Put together your speakers kit – Portfolio, Videos, DVDs, PowerPoint, Photographs, Testimonials

Recommended Monthly Activity

1. Write 5 articles monthly
   - Upload to your website, blog, fan page with a link on your twitter page
   - Distribute to Article Directories
   - Submit to print media

2. Turn your articles into "How To" videos by creating power point and converting it to a slideshow with voice over

3. Upload video to youtube channel and distribute to other video networks

4. Building on the relationship with people on your list, facebook, linkidIn and twitter by sending them the links to the articles, videos send them good content regularly preferably weekly, or fortnightly

5. Explore Joint Venture relationships with other Experts in your Niche

6. Join and Post on forums related to your Brand

7. Set up your promotional monthly campaign

Fast Strategic business plan

Step 1 – Vision – Your destination, where you want to take the business within the next 3 years?

- ..
- ..
- ..

Step 2 – Mission – What is your customer focus for the next 12 months?

- ..
- ..
- ..

Step 3 – Objectives – What is it you have to do to achieve your vision?

- ..
- ..
- ..

Step 4 – Strategy and Tactics – How are you going to execute the objectives?

- ..
- ..
- ..

Step 5 – Projects and action plans – Who is going to achieve them and by when?

- ..
- ..
- ..

The key issue when you have completed your plan is it's achievement; this takes discipline

10 ways to ...grow your business

- Follow these steps to develop your business this year remember
    - **A** – Attention
    - **I** – Interest
    - **D** – Desire
    - **A** – Action

1. Review your business plan. Constant assessment of your approach can help you make the most of new market opportunities. Ask yourself where you want to be in three- to five-years' time and how you can get there. Communicate your strategy to staff — a Government survey found that only a quarter of employees understand their firm's goals

2. Refresh your offer. Make sure your products and services are still fit for your market. Look at your industry and ask what has changed during the downturn. Think about expanding your offer to meet fresh or complementary needs and to keep ahead of your competitors.

3. Maintain your cashflow. Solid finances underpin healthy growth. Update cashflow forecasts and speak to your bank early if you need funds. Accessing bank finance may not be as hard as you expect, as the Government recently extended the Enterprise Finance Guarantee (EFG) scheme.

4. Earn more from existing sales. Focus on selling more to existing high-value clients before investing in finding new customers as it is more cost-effective. Find out what related products or services your customers need; if you can't provide them, refer clients to other suppliers.

5. Target new customers. Relying on existing customers or one or two big clients is risky, so expand your customer base. Set monthly new sales targets and track progress by logging all new sales calls and client meetings and reward staff for hitting targets. Keep abreast of contracts in your sector — Which **5 marketing vehicles** will you use to contact them

6. Open up new channels. Most businesses focus on just one or two sales channels but multiplying your routes to market could reap huge rewards. Sell online if you can, go to trade fairs if appropriate and consider who else could sell your products — existing clients, suppliers, distributors or even businesses with a complementary offer.

7. Be lean and efficient. A cost-conscious mindset will boost your bottom line in the upturn and release resources to plough into growth. Carry out a thorough audit of your overheads; monitor utility bills, shed underperforming suppliers, drop unprofitable product lines and reduce unnecessary staff costs.

8. Promote your business online. Social media marketing will very likely become mainstream in the small business sector. When investing time and money in the likes of Twitter or LinkedIn, however, follow a strategy. There is no "one-size fits all" approach, so make sure what you are doing works — for example, by using web analytics.

9. Reinvigorate your outlook and build new relationships. Even the most committed business owner can become jaded, so make an effort to build new connections with people who can freshen up your thinking or help your business grow. Think about mentors, consultants, new recruits and businesses to form partnerships with. Use on- and offline networks to meet them.

10. Tune into new trends. As the economy picks up, keep your ear to the ground to see what trends you can exploit in your market. Speak to your customers to see how their needs are changing, as well as reading industry news and networking to stay informed.

Recommended Resources

http://www.SimpleInternetBusiness.co.uk   #1 Amazon best-selling Author will show you and teach you how to make money online **for FREE**. Start, Build and **Grow your Own Successful business Online with the help of an internet business mentor.** Learn the Secrets of Successful Internet Marketers who are raking in thousands every month Go To http://www.SimpleInternetBusiness.co.uk

Join the One Million Dollars Club today and learn how to Create Wealth and Streams of Passive Income towards the One Million Dollars goal with multiple step by step strategies go to http://www.OneMillionDollarsClub.com today

www.ingramcontent.com/pod-product-compliance
Lightning Source LLC
Chambersburg PA
CBHW050806180526
45159CB00004B/1568